splinters are children of wood

THE ERNEST SANDEEN PRIZE IN POETRY

Editors
Joyelle McSweeney, Orlando Menes

Editor
John Matthias (1997–2007)

splinters

are

children

of

wood

LEIA PENINA WILSON

University of Notre Dame Press
Notre Dame, Indiana

Published by the University of Notre Dame Press
Notre Dame, Indiana 46556 USA
undpress.nd.edu

Library of Congress Cataloging-in-Publication Data

Names: Wilson, Leia Penina, author.
Title: Splinters are children of wood / Leia Penina Wilson.
Description: Notre Dame, Indiana : University of Notre Dame Press, [2019] |
    Series: Ernest Sandeen prize in poetry
Identifiers: LCCN 2019023573 (print) | LCCN 2019023574 (ebook) | ISBN
    9780268106171 (hardback ; alk. paper) | ISBN 9780268106188 (trade
    paperback ; alk. paper) | ISBN 9780268106201 (pdf) | ISBN 9780268106195
    (epub)
Classification: LCC PS3623.I585483 A6 2019 (print) | LCC PS3623.I585483
    (ebook) | DDC 811/.6—dc23
LC record available at https://lccn.loc.gov/2019023573
LC ebook record available at https://lccn.loc.gov/2019023574

∞ *This paper meets the requirements of ANSI/NISO Z39.48-1992
(Permanence of Paper).*

i do like
how they burn
look at them burn
so many children
look how they burn
those children   that
single hurt color

i do   disobedience
to person   or to poem
undoing person   and poem
undeal all my feelings
i offer you this ruined root—
these pansies—who forfeit beauty for survival—
i promise you can still eat them
this gurl's body

second burial blue memory truetrue feeling dead   finally
finally
dead finally we feast

i fill my own emptiness

tie a ribbon to a tree
leave coconut milk & honey   the white fleece of a young ram
i borrow the best picked men
pick from their bones the best picked women
what's a sentence anyway—prisons
with prisoners' castles

fairytale i know
fairytale i don't
making the labor of arranging words
sacred—i say be
be
be
be
quick—throw tongues into the fire
fill a bloodbowl
offer enough wine
—bathe in the fire—

tell me   are you grieving gurl
r u
r u grieving

gurl
r u
grievinggurl

yes— yes cunt
yes cunt
yes cunt
we sing welcome first earth first mother first morning
each red hibiscus reddens
learning shapeshifting
our bones don't settle—who

do i womb—ha!
who do i woo—woe!
tell me do you believe in resurrection
braiding moon
light into my long braid i do not
flaunt my magic i do not
seek to dwell beastish brutish
banished yet i do love

—who misspells *sacred* missed a spell
scared   scarred
scar red   scathing   cat thing   cared   carried
for whose sake   sake
almost an ache   race   acre   her
are   an insistence of being
reed   read
my spell does not miss—*we carve*
on each other's body
rivers woods   valleys
every evening flower

we carve i am
i am
i am

meaning i am samoan
i am afakasi
i am warrior witch word

we carve the world
the gurl

CONTENTS

AM I THE WORLD OR THE GURL

the world is always burning always burning the gurl always dies always dies am
i the world or the gurl always burning always dying

bury a doll in the shape of myself
i unlife them   over and over
again   again homer's child
plato's child   those forms
foregrounding another's authority
orpheus' head floats off body
off course   i give up
understanding   o mother
receive this prayer—happy cannibalism!

i too fear the heavens   i shear
a lock of my hair   i unutter
god   i fall before you now
a shield

i dig her up   tear her body apart
get at the good meat   redmeat
marrowmeat   heartmeat   womb
i eat   & unmourn

my tongue
hurts into it   manyheaded
manypetaled   many
mistakes   made to say
epic is a wild thing.

she comes too near & feeds from the bodies

into shapes is shaped now her

christmas tree violence ginger man violence reindeer violence

did you know reindeer could be violent all that merry

snow everywhere snow that unwarm moisture the shyness

start fluffing it this prison is very old and prisoning

bee remover pigeon control pink wallpaper with horses and maids—

o it's rowdy so very rowdy

& yet did you know me hands—

i went the fork'd way you showed

my mouth   spat its gravel & yet

when i killed my father i frightened

you   i had only models of ripping

off your clothes & i couldn't

i will not be noisy when you want me to be still i will be glad—

everything lays its corpse but i will not

die i will not repent.

WE CARVE WITHOUT NICETIES HISTORICAL ACCURACY

each man's end is all the cunt for himself.

i lay an iris for each of us who in poverty walks behind eurydice.

combat of beauty and pleasure. probably i won't she says

we were each other's vicious education.   we learned so much

we ruined.   they built monuments to our broken

bones said even our english was broke

a shape of a monster a woman some mal formed skin over

bones over skin over bones

plenty of fatfat   the shape of *make it out alive make it out alive.*

—do we ever

don't be that bitch just behead your lover that learning.

there is a wraith in the birth trees watch out—

i ask the prophet the seer who dreams for dreams too

permit me death too.

i cut my own throat close my own wound wear my own

nightdescended blood.   i will seek aide from my own

enemies if there are friends here hide your eyes.

WE CARVE FROM WHAT WE KNOW
THE REAL LESSON *BELIEVE*

nothing.   sacrifice everything
believe in   nothing
be nothing   how
did you get away with that for so long—we wish
on a shooting star   combine our powers   i do not
want to be lonely   your slick
afterbirth   failed body of
hector   prophetic womanhead   head of
whatever you kill & carry around
this killing your stilled-life   this battle again
again is tiresome   all these old white men
and their same feelings—moon chalice! i want!
to be strong   how will you answer lover! cunt! exile!
the city some dreamydream   again trapped
an imagination limited by that imagination   *i miss*
somehow now weighted against   satisfaction
o grim mouth   grim reaper—just watch me
step into the sea out
of (your) reach   again you think yourself a great original
to have pleased me (once)—what
words will move me
what desire cuts throat to navel   i cut it out

i regret only the intimacy—in the thralls
of the jaws of another afternoon
we demand the other's red—another transformation
rainbow double moon heartache!   or
what dream what maiden what full name
did they stitch you up in
angry dead animal skin
to mirror your angry dead animal soul
rage yet   recognition

i am i am i am

each man's end

an end

and

&

WE CARVE THE ONE WE KNOW

i lay my hand in the wolf's mouth

the wolf knows it will lose its freedom i will lose my hand

we stare at each other like lovers like we don't need freedom or hands

like the sea hasn't risen to welcome us back   like we haven't lost *her*

it's always a her   my island body recoils   as they try to rename me

every mispronounced syllable a papercut   so many papercuts

i die   i try to imagine it hurts less this time   my imagination falters

dropping to one knee i leave blood wonder when it will be used against me

the sea that encloses *her* young body is the sea of many

arms i can't flick what's leftover out

i just rub it in stain it good what fragrance

is this my favorite smell   the blazing secrecy of noon

once more undone it's all pasted underneath my fingernails

underneath the sea where it is dark & muddy & i am blind

underneath the sea where it is dark there is no edge so

sleep my sister   sleep

they feed me this new violence   madonna   un
updated whore—

they make me into a real rat & marvel
my loss of fear

sibyl or unreliable narrator—   my abstract
says something about early 20th century modernism
i don't feel modern   i do feel a machine

they braid purple flowers into my hair & wonder
at its long   its softness
they smell it—*more lavender more lavender*

you will never hear it again they say *the closeness*
of the earth the sky   you will never
see it again they say *those autumn oak leaves*
lose the softness of your sex   here   let me soften you
with sex they do

i can't write this poem   i hate them

is this my epic   wanting all white

men dead   really all men

isn't desire weird   that it expresses
the entire spectrum of human emotion gets me
i think i'm tired   of poetry (is that okay to say)

what am i in possession of really
helen as she desires becomes capable antigone
muscles reacting that time i ate only bread
and milk the beautiful or the terrifying that
icicle   what am i having neither launched 1,000 ships

nor thrown ashes into the air
nor grieved in those ways

there must be different words why else insist—let me

let me learn war   let me learn gathering

one flower two flower three flower   spring flower

unmediated yellow—know me!   sprung

from clouds—calm afternoon clouds

don't you see the winds love me! (frenetic laughter)

don't you see the soil loves me! (a small quake)

they hate you   don't you see even the dumb birds hate you

i can tell you don't see.

i will not award you

for trying to save me from death for dying too

that's so stupid   let me ask you

what would you learn   fully armored

unblushed—spear   & arrow   & (shoulder shrug) guile

yet to take new blood   before someone kills someone kills someone

what would you learn   let me   let me learn *more than survival*

let me learn   that survival

is everything said

in a great voice

                    wait!

is that it really

really

fuck

i am fucked.

the middle

we eat this journey   it's about

consuming again   life   i came

to myself within a dark wood

here the direct way   lost—

could i not possess a city

with my own hands

with my own desire

do i lack everything—

the red sun rises

& i saw you

myself.

WE CARVE WITH RESPECT THE GURL PRAYING

nafanua! ferocious warrior! samoan mother!
thank you for teaching me my power
alofa! alofa! alofa!   yet i am called away

i don't want to go   glittering glittering
athena!   this again   i honor your maternal sinews
every corpse in its place   undreamt melancholy   unhealed

will you let me return
someday   to those volcanic waters

one coin   in one eye
mouth filled with holy dirt   the harvest moon
makes wine of our blood   i drink

the spittle of some bird   offend
the magnificent cow—o
magnificent cow so often i offend!

o comrades! spread your nets   in these woods
i renounce my doubts
holy holy holy—   i will not

run   o bright conflict i do want your body
the deal   she is mine   i save her   i am
an eel   imagining myself a rhinoceros
a wild horse—

a sound sounding   bronzehoofed
gold mane golden thighs golden cunt

don't speak to me
of facts—   i am a bear   a godly bear   the world looks at me

i allow   how vicious devotion
among jackals   that red
gold hunger   i consider all the words i know

unprove them
a pack of hunting dogs approach
i stand
open-armed—

what is it   they say   the extent of women's eru
dition should consist of only simple letters
today she says   i learn   to cut with my cunt
                                 i learn to cut
with my cunt   i learn to
cut with my cunt   i learn to
cut with my cunt   i learn to cut with my cu
nt i learn to cut with my cunt i learn to
cut with my cunt   today i learn to
cut with my cunt   today i learn to
cut with my cunt   today i learn to cut with my cunt   today
i learn to
cut with my cunt   today i learn to
cut with my cunt   today i learn to

      cut with my cunt   today i learn to
      cut with my cunt   today i learn to
      cut with my cunt   cut
      with my cunt cut with my cunt cut with my cunt
                    cut with my cunt cut with my cunt
                    cut with my cunt
        to cut with my cunt to cut with my cunt
        to cut with my cunt to cut with my cunt
        to cut with my cunt to cut with my cunt
        to cut with my cunt to cut with my
        cunt to cut with my cunt to cut with my
        cunt to cut with my cunt to cut with my
        cunt to cut with my cunt
        to cut with my cunt cut with my cunt

cut with my cunt   today i learn to
cut with my cunt   today i learn to
cut with my cunt today i learn to cut with my cunt
today i learn to cut with my cunt to cut with
my cunt to cut with my cunt today i learn to

        cut with my cunt cut with my cunt cut with my cunt
        cut with my cunt

today i learn to cut with my cunt
                              cut with my cunt
today i learn to cut with my cunt
                    to cut with my cunt cut with my cunt cut with my cunt
cut with my cunt cut with my cunt cut with my cunt cut with my cunt cut with
my cunt cut with my cunt cut with my cunt cut with my cunt today i learn to
cunt to cunt to cunt to cunt to cunt to cunt to cunt to cunt to cunt to cunt to
cunt to cunt to cunt to cunt to cunt to cunt to cunt to cunt to cunt to cunt to
cunt to cunt to cunt to cunt to cunt to cunt to cunt to cunt to cunt to cunt to
cunt to cunt to cunt to cunt to cunt to cunt to cunt to cunt to cunt to cunt to
cunt to cunt to cunt to cunt to cunt to cunt to cunt to cunt to cunt to cunt to
cunt to cunt to cunt to cunt to cunt to cunt to cut with my cunt to cut with my
cunt to cut with my cunt to cut with my cunt to cunt to cunt to cunt to cunt to
cunt to cunt to cunt to cunt to cunt to cunt to cunt to cunt to cunt to cunt to
cunt to cunt to cunt to cunt to cunt to cunt to cunt to cunt to cunt to cunt to
cunt to cunt to cunt to cunt to cunt to cunt to cunt to cunt to cunt to cunt to
cunt to cunt to cunt to cunt to cunt to cunt to cunt to cunt to cunt to cunt to
cunt to cunt to cunt to cunt to cunt to cunt to cunt to cunt to cunt to cunt

a hot game
your tongue   my mouth   unmangled
                    and folded over
                            teeth glow

        men are driven mute
        the dragon's charlatan comes and goes   such prophecy

            hedges are set ablaze the harvest burned-off
            parts of hercules are flammable   the fires burn them away

                cover your body too   here   use these ashes   i
                    who was a daughter am now a son

                        my own end—failure of permission
                        or is it ownership

                    heavy head
                            heavy arms heavy hands

                                    the epic
                                    lets death in   she screams
                                            her mother mourn
                                            or is worn out

                        to eat the sun every night & give birth

                        the screaming brat's a sheep
                                    shaking a bush
                                o where

                    o where o
                    where is the noon   we waited
                        we are young   what blood
                                    is there
                                        left.

what can affect
the conflict
dis   course
that discursive horse
if you break its legs
it won't be able to run
it will just die there
slowly
in pain
what else   i like
the sound of
that distress.

am i
to be
relieved of
this life

—or returned

i saw
a rabbit

caught in
its own

deathsoundbodywilt
a plea
really—o

please o
please o   please o
please o please o please o please stop

some untranslatable *killmeplease*

killmeplease
killmeplease

killmeplease
killmeplease

killmeplease
killmeplease

killmeplease
killmeplease

killmeplease
killmeplease

killmeplease
killmeplease

killmeplease
killmeplease

killmeplease
killmeplease

killmeplease
killmeplease

killmeplease
killmeplease

killmeplease
killmeplease

killmeplease
killmepl
ease

there is no need for you

approach me   you will die   take courage if you near

we all die

i ate her liver and became her

i ate her cunt and understood

o—o—*o*   the difficult task of knowing—

we are all ambitious

we all hate one another

the road gives way

must the road give way

WE CARVE A PROPHECY

we are sleeping

we sit naked together

do not speak

do not smile politely

do not make eye contact

do not look   at ourselves

we devour

we   achilles   barefoot

scourge of cities   hard

loved   we are not less cold

the nearby river is dirty

the moon does not reflect here

we cannot get our hands clean

can i still touch you

help me   am i not your son

help me   goddess of this sea   my mother

would that i could love you better would i

silence   silent   silent

contemplation   o loss!

even the sun refuses

to clothe our hands!

WE CARVE A PROPHECY *THE WORLD OR THE GURL*

i denounce *that*
i might not have learned my own tongue but mother
says it's in the blood   & i am willing
i will not share your bed though i may grow old
if you sleep while the sun is down you might dream (of me)
(you might die)

& am i   pulled away   or let go
                    —some horses' bitch   here
                            is a romance as old as time

& are you mourning too   my loss or yours
do you hold my body tender   or trophy

& baby   if you could see my face
                    you'd write a poem   (i would)
ask too   why does love love life
                    & death
                            for the sake
                            of its own meaning
lackofgreenness   i denounce that too
& i want you
                    to die first   that's the meanness of it
                    human life is so ordinary!

            we know nothing we know nothing we know
                    nothing we know
                    nothing
& can know nothing   i deny myself
what voices i borrow
                    what god was
                    like—what god is
daughter your foot is tragic!   now come! & dance
        with me!   tell me what you want

all i want is to eat live eat live eat
& eat
& live
& all i want is for there to be no shame here
& here
& here
& here

besides the serpents mother also sent venom from the hydra   hallucination
blindness   rage   bloodlust   all ground finely into a powder
mixed with fresh blood her blood to a boil
everything must come to a boil inside a great bronze kettle
settled into the earth covered with hot rocks ocean rocks
and coconut fronds tightly woven
and whatever else you might like for dinner
mother always careful what was for friend what was foe
so she stirs with a fresh wand from the hemlock tree
& she grinds it until it is
so so fine fine
massages it into our bodies makes us deadly makes us deadly you cannot touch
me i am
untouchable   deadly
& full

you're such a fool.

WE CARVE A SPELL *GURL*

i never see light i learn the dark
there is ringing   the ringing is nothing
there is knocking   the knocking is nothing
i'm emblossomed still i see no thing
that dark i beat
so hard i splinter
i burn so brightly
burn myself away
the sun stood halfway
between the night driven off
and the night newly approaching
bodies shed
garments
o how they glisten
o how they glisten.

WE CARVE A SPELL *GURL*

naked nymphs beat their breasts & fill the clearing with shrill & startled cries

WE CARVE A SPELL *GURL*

she interrupted erupts   wants the one thing to which there never is   enough
she does not know that thing   whatever death is she is nervous about it
there is a road
darkened on all sides by funeral yew trees   boneless bodiless shades stray
here
sluggish styx waits   that everybody river exhales
cuntfucking one wasteland into another wasteland
souls newly come are at a loss to find & yet
& yet
&

WE CARVE A SPELL *GURL*

she exposing he
rself for what she is
both paternal & perv
erse captures the maiden
's baffled father

cuts him

WE CARVE *USO* SISTER TO SISTER

to sister   another spell *sister*

i don't
want martyrdom
my heart
beats too

mean yet   i imagine
the swordsman fell

in love
let's settle this
without the need
to grieve brothers'
body   or watch
old men fall to old men knees

i make no apologies
smooth rocks heat while we wait we
hack the small limbs off
bigger kindling   separate the leaves

        coconut taro banana   braid the fish into it
        i tuck a piece of your hair behind your ear
        you've cut it   this imagination
        isn't mine anymore   how to imagine out of it

we talk over each other raze each other
that's our way how to
find our way again please
pass the palusami   please sit crossed legged and talk to us
please leave your shoes at the door   mother says
if we work hard we can eat sooner
she stitches with ink the chimera's
image onto my left tit
when it's too much she says cut yourself wild again
let the ocean back out

                                        is it worse   to return empty
                                                    or not at all

in the poems we all die just another way poetry reflects life another way a woman
is made i mean marginalized i mean we lose intimacy i mean i want each loyalty
tested can you tell me why hope is always blind is it the world she sits on or some
floating inflatable toy i mean if *if* i let all the air out will i die from that air   or
drown by plastic aesthetic i mean is this all there is to know about connection
did you really just ignore my text   mother always said if you break it it will come
true i break a gurl's body   is it true

            i select
            a torch
            steeping in
            blood not
            yet my
            own   put on
                    my robe
                    of dripping gore
                    and a belt
                    of live snakes   & so appareled i set out
                    from home   & so appealing i set out from home

the flesh
of her poetface
gurl   world
some other malady   i pull
down
make it my mask   mine.

now i drive my cart
plow my plow

i recognize my vertigo   redness   deeply alien
the faithless eye between us
ungathered meadows tendering dawn
                       fill a ditch
                       with blood   drive ghosts away
                       that smell
                                 nationality
                                 something in each of us waits
                                 to see the other survive

severed   she says this casually
what face
lets itself be looked at.   what face
can help it.
i give away
my mother.   mother! wound!
will it be enough   bring my horn
my valkyries!
vengeance   avenged
o to kill
the killers!

this skull helen's.

this skull marguerite's.

this skull matilda's.

this skull marianne's.

this skull beatrice's.

this skull gertrude's.

this skull audre's.

this skull mary's.

this skull virginia's.

this skull vera's.

this skull nora's.

this skull diane's.

this skull elizabeth's.

this skull gloria's.

this skull alice's.

this skull cathy's.

this skull kathy's.

this skull robin's.

this skull jane's.

this skull leia's.

where's your skull.

show me yours.

does my cunt

make you

feel good

WE CARVE THE LEARNING OUT

carefully

you trained me

to care about this   *ikeepyou   youkeepme*

we are each *kept*—

i open the body of your newest dog with my own teeth.

i hope you loved it   i hope you loved it and weep now for that loss.

tell me truthfully

is my only choice—lover! cunt! exile!

must this be love / must i love

or some other bird   it's always a bird isn't it
fuck a bird   a poem
            pigeon   eaten out by rat   saved you
                        an eye   what
                        an inheritance   from sacred earth
                        to trash-day-monday   the words
                                                too many
                                                wounds inherited
                                                i guess
            i'll just
            run off   & fall in love
                        with a centaur

            anything can be sacred   i guess
            nothing is

WE CARVE THE SPELL *GURL* AS MANY TIMES
AS NEEDED

o horrible tenderness! battle sweat! it's noon!
crinkled wings sour everyman's face   patroclus
underlines   you are not alone
lonely   without criticism
      lovethings are whispered
      let me pace
      without fear   the common path
      of death.
            true spring plants chains!   profoundest
            sense! city shame!
            almost palatable daffodils!
            blackblack horses!
            new achilles
            wears the horns of a ram
                        for luck   her family letters *here*
                        for luck   become a god yourself
                        say this prayer *guard me against*
                                  guard against me she says
                                  this world is falling in love
                                  i have robbed myself
                                  what god opposes me
                                  i do not know.

WE CARVE FROM WHAT'S LEFT
OF THIS WORD *GURL*

she o unfair she o stop your weeping that ugly face
with her hand she stretches forth to mine
a sickle
unloves my failure
this fright that kept me up at night
stay away with me.

i press my body over her wildness
          as close to the bone as though she were my own skin
     we wrestle
          color overcomes us   that foul cry might have gotten louder
                              out of hand   yet hadn't

mock-orange horses
        pull a chariot aspiring to rule
                the heavens

                    & always sudden the door
                    new eternity irises
                    before me   my heart knows   i pray

            i may never die   nor surrender
        nor modesty taint me

i love you   i have
        the disguise of love
        though mother may never recognize me   again
        so i sew a black dress
        throw it over myself
        throw it over the dawn throw it over the dawn throw it over the dawn.

I APPEAR SEEKING REVENGE FOR THE DESTRUCTION OF THOSE CHILDREN

but this exquisite—

re: this exquisite wetness.

what now—

re: when i have *tried* and failed i shall have failed.

high summer is over i return to the sleeping place will you return with me—

re: the wound.

am i allowed to win—

re: the same death the live rabbit formed in rupture are wildthings.

all the doors of truth are open now to battle—

re: hold my hand do not let go we will take each other run away with the other.

all i ever wanted, you, myself—

re: i want.

how do the promise of heaven and the brokenness of earth correspond—

re: it will rain tonight.

will i have to kill (you) can i—

re: hold my hand i will steady you.

are you aphrodite, ares—a ghost, some god—

re: what can i know the dandelions have already dispersed.

i do not remember if only—

re: do not remember.

they killed her—

re: yes.

i hate them—

re: yes.

i will murder them—

re: yes.

i will not weep for it—

re: do not weep for it.

what can i give you—

re: what will i not take.

if this catastrophe is eternal—

re: it's located in my body, yours, do not forget i will make you fiercest.

will i find you when it's all over—

re: i will shed blood for it.

is it always permanent red can we breathe in all that red—

re: we will bathe in it.

i do fear—

re: i die by my own hand.

did we ever recognize each other—

re: i will cut you mark you.

let us be brave—

re: let us be badass.

YOU MUST ALWAYS FEED
FROM THE BODIES

you must always feed from the bodies

grandmother   i refuse love i sin
weeping with earth's knife i drop
this body   and empty
myself
horror   here! i! am!
our blood unrecognizes
each other   the other
skinloud
boneloud eyeloud
this moon   your body
what's left of it   griefdream—to know
i survived first: loyalty
you've grown
uglier
your hands covered with cuts—

                each a long and short vowel
              it's time   ta'ei
     ta'ei   —fe'ai   —fe'ai
          a   e   i   o   u
     fa
  ga la mo nu
       pi sa ti

  vi

      o no wildness thieved i'll speak / in english
to every awe

                  & embarrassment—

o most gifted eye do not

see the banality of this world

see only what grace lent

in unwise pegasus   all eight

wings of the seraphim

avenge our grief   what is left

what i believe

a skull falls to earth   i carry

it around   show it the world   here

here   green proud hummingbird

fervor pinked sky   here

cicadas have swarmed

turtle is full

moths have lived

two days   pine marten plays

eats squirrel

mountain bones crumble

worn down by ice

the sudden erosion of a seabed: why

i murdered you   the power

of suggestion   of inflection

of invocation   let me

have you

let me

have you

let me

have you

let me

have you

let me

have you

let me

have

tenderness—

teeth—

because   other mother   i see

your body   boarbody   sharkbody   the garden

wounds   the hunt or the hurt   what bends (to)

an idea   fire or word—   what have i forgotten as a poet

of the empire   *or*—

what narrow shame

what can i know a part from

the plot—

what can i know

take me back

take me back   take

my body   slowly

into the sea

slowly into the sea   don't leave me

here

don't leave me here   please take

my body back into the sea

however slowly

slowly / a favorite lover's kiss

the first leaf of each new tree after the snow melts

or joy

slowly / joy

mother's dark hair   her

sharpsharp tongue   odin's right eye gifted

grown from sacred vines

that temper   i inherit

all green mischief   i queen

of poem

performing humility

tear the roots up

denounce what will heal   will heal

each petal falls

each sounds woe

echo   the clearing

thrilled cunts

and we are thrilled

and we are cunts   in true friendship

i sing   in griefsong

shed grieftears

shed griefsweat   here

drink   rage

rage

rage

rage (against the dying)

i live it   knowing   no mother

forced to translate the self out

white dress blue stockings first soul   be mother

hold me   we must

love each other or die

i take a shower   keep the mating ground clean

i eat i earn i rid   in spring i open every window

too suddenly   the lungs   grasping

each day

you are mean   i must

guilt   our building

unwitnesses our love

she weighs her heart against a fat rabbit

o pure heart   your romance unreliable

gathering the lost parts of her brother   she makes him

her hippopotamus

her love   face contorting

i seal my heart

in the belly

of a great reptile

everyday   i feed it

everyday   throw it meat

pour water on its great green head

wipe smut from its early morning eyes

ou te alofa ia te oe   i tell it

i promise   alofa ia te oe

i win the heart   of a good goat
place it at your feet

i have undone the evildoer   mother
lay claim to this world

with closed lips drink this world

how willful these lips!
all men drop their own name!

i find achilles hiding among women
and make a prettypretty dress
out of his leanlean skin

i confess i love   almost
successfully   this day's sun cleanses
who i was   the great danger
i might die
without

find my clean self
smear mud on my red gold horns—

stand mouth open   my own
animal   i prepare clean wine   cakes
baked into the shapes of other animals
to show gratitude

i know i will die terribly—

—what social inheritances don't
baffle   o sweet eel

long toothed devil   i know your loyalty   still

do not weep   mother   you have taught me
my own name
how to weigh my bones
death   anyway

let's smile at what wealth
my new nostrils   these necessary
nearnesses *i love you*
also *this is my revenge*

mother mother mother mother mother i murmur

i am your most fierce

warrior   mother do what

you will with me

i will do what you will

myself   an animal

no spot or stain

no truer body   giving thanks

to the sacred fish   at last

i arrange my kills

to control the soliloquy

that solitary distrust

my impatience   all skulls

neatly forward

my real self   all tender

tender red

protect my priestesses'

enemies from their failure

fill them with arrows   preserve

what goodness they offer   put their

useful parts in jars   lungjar

liverjar kidneyjar

when they are accustomed

to their suffering   i will teach them

it is real   madness   on my knees

i approach love

i hold   i repeat   hold   repeat

hold

all the bells say

too late   morning sun cuts

goats from an evergreen forest   my sisters flee   not wholly

animal   their voices untimely

frost   seeding error   say *ferocious*

is the centipede   say i pretend

understanding   say do not let go   mother!

your blood calls to me

my samoan blood!

i drink   redden myself   stand

horned   obey the storm's wet

i leave fruit   my love

the soft underbelly of many foxes

mother   i can speak to birds and

trees and blossoms

these orange flowers are their own evident

exaltation

my syntax mistakes   i wrap myself in a coat

given to feeling   i cry

o heart living by death

o noble temper tell me the word

that makes my heart groan   o call

not me to wound this wrong   the bluest

blueterror   call not me for i am of

endless night and know no

sweet delights

baby let me

tell you some secret you

already

                              no.   every secret

                              already wild. don't

                              take it

                              tame. i don't

                              want

                              just

                              any fight. do i

                              want

a pretty pink man-o-war

washed up on shore   don't

touch

      touch   & you'll never

make it home

sometimes the sea gives

                              sometimes she

                              takes

   i won't

   warn you

   (again)

how do i know

what you have

taken away   in the next book i will

know what i know about death

i will know what i know about affection

o guardian beast how often

my affection

falters!

i will know what i know about resisting

the meaning   whatever

it is that means   yet here

right now   sing—

sing with me—

either closer to hell or further from

can we   sisters   be   as beautiful

as   too much of a good thing

as   i feel so deeply

there's something in the air

o overripe banana!   you heel!

bursting—bursting—bursting—to

burst forth   from underneath

could i leave it all behind mother

could i just fall away / an evening fog

the tide coming in and out

shadows flickering   stretching towards—descending—

the descent i'm

tired of it

a violence or a love

me love me not love me love me not love me love me not lo

lo—lo—   & behold!

she kills a bear

eats its heart   takes its strength

there's pleasure here & an inability to communicate

as if it took more than a moment to figure out the kill   or

to come to terms with such live threshing   or

she couldn't bring herself to it   yet wet evidence

the ooey-gooey between her toes   blushing footprints   i dream

there's snow   the snow is dirty   nothing is out of sight

nothing is escapable—

would that this were sand—less traceable witness

suddenly it's all so immortal   so what

she makes a talisman of its lung—may i too

breathe clearly this winter   unslept

may i too be so full—

the next day   superstition or love or

she offers it to her sisters

here eat my heart

take this strength   be so full

baby am i master

of what

i speak   that is

poetry

    undescent—   (is it indecent)

    light, wound

    glistening, dusk   am i

          going to write   the grammar

          whose tongue is   death

          or immortality

ah! AGAIN THESE CHOICES

did i love you   (did i ever!)

profound belief   vibrant coral

the moth knows luxury

is such a human thing

mother gave me this body

this fine and useful life

today i return these parts to mother

the mirror of my heart reflects so softly the horror   false

experience   why do i recall your bones

mother rejects my first conclusion my fifth

she rejects my forwardness my affection

lionheaded mother   it's upon us

do you hear it   such delicate sounds

really   brother

you must always feed

from the bodies

i did love you   against my every

domestic fear   sounds like *domination*

sister your plastic lover pollutes our oceans

if it isn't sustainable it will kill you

he will kill all of us

i love you

i am willing

to do this killing   sister! mother! i bundle

wild sage chamomile my own

glimmering body safely put away

for just an occasion   now pass me

the bloodbowl i offer it to you full

swear an oath

i boil the silkworm   remove its body

steal its silk   for the pyre

for you   mother   i will restore you

even the first blue crocus

of spring   which i have kept safe

i burn

take your bloodsong

into myself

i sing

unattach my/self from the divine

am divine   world— does it mean   *course of anyone's life*

mean *forgive me these trespasses*

mean *forgive these worldly ways*   heavy reading is not

the same as heavy petting   if only   do not worry mother

i have not lost sight—i place my good eye

at the trunk of the oldest tree   i mix

my mixed blood into the wings

my afakasi blood   i make

the pegasus red-winged—set her free

no need to escape—what state

of disorder   is there some worse

form of life than this mirror-of-steel

uninsistence—

i didn't notice the horse-backed rider

i fail us

all my goats are dead

i wash their still

soft heads   tear open

the darkness   learn its

alphabet   the rich soil

is not a dead thing

my goats shed their skin

i shed my own cocoon

the fresh skin   no longer

jove's costume

i dance

deliberately

smack the earth

with my bare feet

an occasion a quickening

brother

beat the drum for me

o unlearned feelings! crisis! do not

lament   the last yellow

petals of spring have

fallen   chasm!   rupture!

        what sacrifice will turn

        your head   already

        my daughter learns her image

        records the way she looks

                whenever she looks at herself

                repeats her image   dirty satyr!

                i weep for slights

                insults unavenged

vengeance! come!

here! i am dangerous

here! gone mad

here! gone home   mother!

        all-mother!   i'm so scared i imagine immediate

        red   immediate red immediate red

        destroyer of the vine   i imagine

        the bow   bent   evil

        faced two ways

        twice broken   reaving

i keep the wound   open

uncovered   to take refuge

wolves winter over   my fear my womb

feeds itself   makes me a knife   most delicate pearl

layered treasure sunken each anemone sacrificing their desire—

layered angler-fish-glow deep sea camouflage deep sea poison—

each gesture most delicate blue braided into

blade   what violent delightfulness

keeping the home safe keeping the plot—sever

divine recollections—nature is

all imagination—a knife (always a knife)   electric eel

some fruit to peel   some formless faith—a knife

to open the coconut a pomegranate

a knife-blade to explore the wreck

a knife to vicious those blood-loving bats in all their viciousness

a knife-blank   cannot recollect when it belongs (it's all in pain)

a knife-still   loaded still roaming the seas   still hunting the golden doe

taking my clothes off i fold myself in front of her

lay my lips to her hooves my neck to her nose her teeth

ask if she will hide me   or take me back into the sea

do not she says   i will not

renounce my knife for a blanket

nor forget my ordinary fear   of course

there will be a time to eat

do not be tardy

desiring body   devouring body

green great island   o sanctuary

do not gape! i live

anxiously   o hollow

hades   disaster unburies

all   i eat

every day   i am human

i do sorrow

always it's fear me

       revere me

       worship me   stupid

   love!   stupid beauty!

  hasty! so very hasty

       i dream   so smitten   dark named

       destiny seizes grandmother

       carries her off   terrified

          i hear her cry out for

her mother her kin

       but for her mother most often

i leave this mistletoe for mother

i surrender

the world   all its worldly ways

my braveness   deep

rooted and animal

these wounds

i inflicted on myself

these are mine!

lightning!   rescue

or ruin!   mother

your strict white blossoms

my own shelter

into my thigh brother

tattoos my body whole

tap tap tap

a shield   poison

from the jaws of cerberus   tap tap

tap centipede   fish

sphinxes' riddle—refrain

renews itself   the art of respect

renews itself—renews

a chimera's wet   ruby   lust   wine-dark—tap

tap—we emerge

healed from salted water

we begin—we begin: who

who wishes to walk

with me will prove

already too late

i hung all the mistletoe

i speak unsaid password—tap

tap tap

i thirst   the whole

bird's life   a wildness

of dawn   i score

the palm of my foot with a stone

set the stone on an altar   sharp

definition   grandmother

welcomes all righteous dead

i give tangerines for my fortune

hear my voice!

see my face!   taste

for the first time my mouth!

unblind!

END NOTES & DEBTS
(OF LOVE)

These spells are directly in response to, and in some cases use the language of, the following fellow casters: Alice Notley, Anne Waldman, Gertrude Stein, Marianne Moore, Robert Hass, Sophocles, Virginia Woolf, Sylvia Plath, HD, Mina Loy, Homer, Robin Blaser, W. H. Auden, Adrienne Rich, Djuna Barnes, William Carlos Williams, T. S. Eliot, Kathy Acker, Dylan Thomas, Naoko Takeuchi, Emily Brontë, Emily Dickinson, Euripides.

LEIA PENINA WILSON

is an afakasi Samoan poet hailing from the Midwest.
Her work has appeared in *Dream Pop Press, Split Lip,
Birdfeast, Bombay Gin, Powder Keg,* and *OmniVerse.*
She is the author of *i built a boat with all the towels
in your closet (and will let you drown),* winner of the
2012 To the Lighthouse Poetry Prize.

CPSIA information can be obtained
at www.ICGtesting.com
Printed in the USA
LVHW110030270819
629056LV00002B/343/P

9 780268 106188